Mom, how come I'm not thin?

ISBN 0-89638-044-0

Mom, how come I'm not thin?

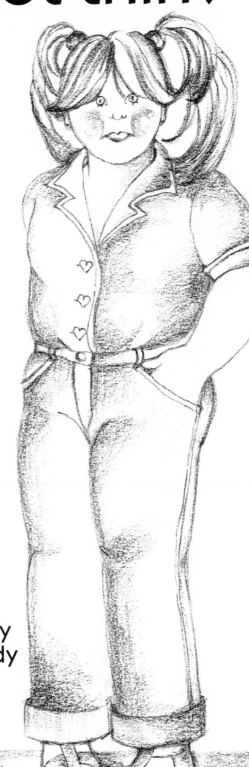

Bill & Enid
Bluestein

Illustrations by
Susan Kennedy

Published by
CompCare
publications
Minneapolis, Minnesota
A division of Comprehensive Care Corporation

Our thanks to the fellowship of Overeaters Anonymous, especially those who shared their stories and, in their sharing, gave us the inspiration to put into words their childhood years and their eventual successes.

To Lisa, our dear little friend,
with much love and deep appreciation.

When my mother was a little girl, she had a favorite doll she always played with. When she grew up and I was born, she decided I would be her special doll. So you know what she named me? Dolly.

When I was a baby, I had these round rosy cheeks and chubby little legs. Everyone said I looked cute. I guess in a way I really did look like a doll then. Now I'm not happy with my name because as far as I'm concerned, I sure don't look like a doll anymore. I still have round cheeks and my legs are still chubby, but on someone in the fifth grade that's not pretty. That's called being fat!

Sometimes I feel as if I'm the only one in the whole world who's fat. I know that's not true, but nobody I know really well has my problem.

Take the people in my family...Now my dad has lots of muscles. He's always exercising and he looks great. He used to play football when he was in high school. My mom is pretty thin, but she's always trying to lose a little weight in her hips. She's always dieting on and off, but she can hide her weight by dressing very carefully. I can't hide my weight. The only way I could do that would be to wear a tent over my head. You see, I'm not thin ANYWHERE.

My brother Andrew, who is a big deal in junior high school, is super thin. He can eat everything and anything all the time and he never gets fat. I mean never!

If I just look at what he's eating, I gain weight. There are moments when I get very, very jealous. I even hate him sometimes. There are times when I really feel sorry for myself and think that life is very unfair. I especially think so when Andrew is eating a piece of chocolate cake. He is a chocolate nut!

I'm considered very smart in school. I always get very high grades. Andrew isn't so smart. He's always getting C's and D's. Mom and Dad really get mad at Andrew, but then again, every once in a while my dad makes excuses for him and says, "Well, at least he is a terrific athlete." You know what? If I could trade my brains for Andrew's thin body, I'd gladly give up being smart. I really would.

I sometimes think Andrew is embarrassed being with me. He's really friendly when we're at home, but when we're out together—which isn't very often—I sometimes feel that he walks a little bit ahead of me, just so no one thinks we're together. I always have to run to keep up with him. It's very hard.

I know he loves me though. I remember the time when Big David down the block called me "fatso" and I started to cry. I was very young then, so I cried. I don't cry out loud anymore when people call me names, but I do cry when nobody can see me.

Anyway, Big David called me "fatso" and Andrew actually said, "Don't you call my sister 'fatso'!"

Big David said, "Why not? That's what she is."

Well, Andrew— you should have seen him! Andrew started to hit him. The problem was that Big David is REALLY big and Andrew is not so tall. Big David picked Andrew up and threw him in the bushes. Thank goodness Andrew only got scratched up a little, but you know what? Big David didn't call me names anymore.

That was a long time ago, and now Big David is pretty grown up and, in my opinion, Big David has become Fat David.

Even though I like school, there are times I wish I didn't have to go. Boys can really be mean. There's this boy Jason—he sits next to me—who says, "Hi, Chubby," every morning. That's how my day starts and that hurts my feelings a lot. I ignore him, but not really. I always get a little pain in my stomach after he says those words.

One time Jason was called up to the front of the room. When he walked by me, I stuck out my foot and tripped him. No one noticed that I did it and Jason fell right on his face. His nose started bleeding and all the kids laughed at him. He was very embarrassed and had tears in his eyes. A part of me was really happy I did that, and a part of me was really sad for him. I really don't like to act mean, but sometimes I do because I get so angry I don't know what to do.

Most of the kids in my class say that recess is their favorite subject. It's the one I hate the most. That's when most of the boys in my class call me names. I feel so embarrassed and angry at the same time. When I try to tell the teacher—who is, of course, thin—all she ever says is, "Try to ignore them." Let me tell you, it's impossible to ignore a bunch of boys calling you names. It is REALLY impossible! I wish I could press a button and become six feet tall with muscles, just for recess, just one time...

The problem is...I feel so bad when the boys are mean that when I come back to class it's hard to start on my school work. Who can think about spelling when you've been called names for the past half hour?

I do have some nice girl friends, but none of them are fat like me. Even though I like them and I know they like me, I never tell any of them how I feel. I like my friends, but I guess I don't trust them. I mean, what would I do if I told people my feelings and they made fun of me? Or worse yet, what would I do if they told everybody else what I said? I think I would die. So I keep my feelings inside.

When I see the older girls in my school looking at me and they smile, I just know what they're thinking and I feel awful. When some of the girls in my class look at me and talk to each other, I know what they're thinking, too—"Dolly is fat and funny-looking."

Half the kids in my class eat healthy lunches—no junk food. The other half of my class could care less. They are always bringing Twinkies or Ding Dongs in their lunch bags. My luck...I sometimes end up eating right next to Monica Harris or Roger Schwartz. They always have cake, cookies, or cupcakes, usually my favorite kinds. I just don't understand how they can stay so thin. Like I said before, it's not fair!

Speaking of cupcakes, I once had a very embarrassing thing happen to me. The PTA was having a bake sale at our open house. For bake sales, all the mothers make a lot of delicious treats. They sell them and the money goes to our school. School was almost over and my teacher asked me to run an errand for her down by the main office. On the way there, I had to pass the cafeteria where some of the mothers were putting out the food. There on one of the tables were the prettiest chocolate cupcakes. They had all different colored sprinkles on top. I just couldn't help myself. They looked so good. It was as if the cupcakes were talking to me. I put out my hand (it should have fallen off!) and started to take the one at the very corner of the table. Just as my hand went around the cupcake one of the mothers, Mrs. Sullivan, screamed out, "Dolly, what are you doing?" I just froze. And Mrs. Sullivan said in an even louder voice, "Young lady, get your hands off that cupcake!"

Just as she said it, Mrs. Frazier's class walked into the hallway. "I'm sorry," I answered and suddenly I started crying, and I ran down the hall as fast as I could, but not fast enough. I could hear all the kids laughing. I swore then that I would never eat another cupcake again, but I have.

My mother is always putting me on diets which never work. When I bring my diet food to eat, someone—usually one of the boys—says something about it. I don't like it when people call me "Dolly the Rabbit" or say things like, "If you eat like a bird, how come you don't look like a bird? Ha ha ha." When they do it too much, I really lose my appetite sometimes. I wish that would happen more often. See, sometimes when everyone makes fun of me, I go home and eat everything I can get my hands on. When I feel the most unhappy, the only thing that makes me feel good is food. Then after I eat I feel even worse. But I still can't stop eating.

I don't like physical education either! I think the next time Mr. Dobson decides to have relay races, I am going to fake a faint. I really am! Mr. Dobson picks captains for each team, and then the captains get to pick the ones they want on their team. I usually get picked last. The captains always groan when they see I'm stuck on their team. Now the last time we had relay races, our team was really good—except for me, of course. I was the last one to run on the team, and I was way in the lead because I started out before everyone else. That was because the rest of our team was so fast.

I was really trying my best, and suddenly Robin Gerber caught up with me. And before I knew it, so did Bobbie Sullivan. And then Richard passed me by. And then everyone did and I came in last. My team really hollered at me. They called me names ("fatso" was one of them), and I felt so bad I just didn't know what to do. Mr. Dobson gave a big lecture on how everyone should be a good sport and it's just a race, etc., but it didn't make any difference—it was too late. I think that was one of the worst days of my life.

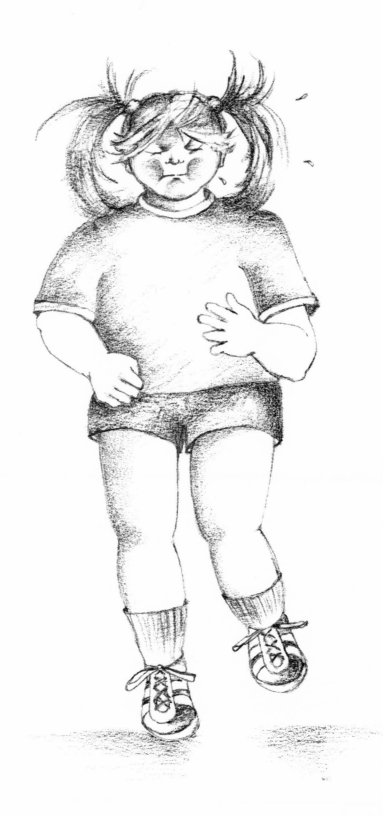

When I came home from school that day, I was a wreck. My mother noticed and said, "Why, Dolly, what's wrong? You look just terrible! What happened?" I started crying (I promised myself I wasn't going to cry anymore, but I did) and I told her what happened.

She said, "You'll see, honey. You'll lose weight and then everything will be all right. I just read about a brand new diet and we're going to go shopping and get the right food for the diet."

Now as I said before, I know she feels bad for me. I can see the look in her eyes, but I wish she would have said, "Dolly, I can understand why you feel so bad. That must have been terrible. Come here—let me just hold you for a little while." I know that's what she was thinking, but I sure wish she would say it. Maybe then I could talk to her about how bad I feel a lot of times. I get so lonely.

I hate the word "diet." All diets do is make me think about food more than ever. No one else I know except for adults ever goes on diets, and most of the adults I know who go on diets always put their weight right back on. When I go on diets, I usually wind up cheating, and then I feel bad about that. When I cheat on my diet, my mother can tell. Like the time I kissed her and she could smell chocolate on my breath. "Dolly, do I smell chocolate? Dolly, did you eat some candy? Dolly, I'm so disappointed in you." What can you say when someone says that?

One time my mom said good-by and left to go shopping. After she closed the door, I went into the bread drawer to get a piece of bread. Just as I had the bread in my hand...there was my mother. She had forgotten her car keys. She looked at me, and I looked at her, and neither one of us said a word. Sometimes when people say nothing, it's worse than when they say something.

I remember asking my mother once, "Mom, how come I'm not thin?" She told me that it probably had to do with heredity. She explained that mothers and fathers have something called genes, and when they make a baby these genes decide if you're going to be short or tall, blue-eyed or brown-eyed, light-skinned or dark-skinned—even fat or thin. She told me that she had some relatives that had weight problems, and my father did, too. So she probably had some of the genes in her and my father probably had some of these genes in him, and they both gave them to me. She also told me there is no way to pick and choose the genes you get. It's all just one big surprise. What a surprise! That's like saying, "Surprise! You've got the measles or poison ivy!"

If I'm down the block and Mrs. Cooper gives me a cookie (Mrs. Cooper bakes the best chocolate chip cookies I've ever tasted), I can almost hear my mother sighing, even though she's not there. I know it really bothers her that I'm not thin. She loves me, but I guess if I were a mother and had a fat daughter and no one else had a fat daughter, well—I guess that would bother me, too. I feel a lot of pressure.

I know it bothers my father, too. He doesn't talk a whole lot—he's the silent, handsome type, but I bet secretly he wouldn't mind my being so big if I were a boy. If I were a boy, maybe I could be a football player like he was. Maybe then my dad would be proud of me.

A long time ago Andrew told me that he thought that my dad really was expecting to have another son. Andrew told me that when my mother was pregnant with me, my dad used to tell him that one day he'd have a brother to play ball with. I guess I disappointed him.

When my mom took me to the doctor, I asked him why I wasn't thin. I told him my mother explained about heredity, but I wanted to hear his opinion. He said, "Dolly, your mother is partially right, but sometimes it also has to do with what you eat and how much you eat. We measure our weight in pounds and our height in inches. We count our food in calories. For instance, a piece of chocolate cake has hundreds of

calories, and lettuce hardly has any calories at all. If what you eat adds up to a lot of calories, then you gain weight, and if you eat very few calories, then you lose weight.'' He gave me a big lecture on eating the right foods and all that stuff. I think I am sorry I asked him. It's very confusing.

When my cousin Caroline got married, I was invited to the wedding. My parents really thought that was terrific, because my aunt and uncle were afraid she was never going to get married. Caroline is nice, but she's kind of strange.

I didn't have anything to wear. My dress-up dress was too tight, so my mother told me she would buy me a new dress. Next to relay races and recess, I hate shopping. Oh, don't get me wrong—I love pretty clothes, but I hate stores.

Most of the girls in my class wear jeans and T-shirts. I love jeans, but it's very hard to find a pair that fits me right. Sometimes if they don't fit right, they cut into my legs and hurt, so my mother usually buys me dresses. They hide my fat better.

I'll never forget one time I did wear my jeans to school and when I bent down to pick up my notebook on the floor, I heard this terrible sound. It was the sound of the seat of my pants ripping. It's a sound I'll never forget. I had to walk backwards to my seat, and my mother had to bring me something else to wear. Oh, well, just one more embarrassing moment in the life of Dolly the Fat!

If I were thin, I think I'd like to be a fashion model. When no one is looking, I sometimes look in the bathroom mirror and make model faces. It's fun.

I almost always take a sweater to school with me, because then I can put it on my lap and hide my stomach. Or when I walk home, I can hold it in front of me, and then I don't feel as fat.

I like rainy weather the best because everyone wears a raincoat. When everyone wears a raincoat, they look the same because raincoats are so big.

When I go shopping, I always start out in the "seven-to-fourteen" section, but I never seem to be able to find anything that fits me. That makes me feel really bad, especially when the salesgirls suggest I try a different department like the "chubby" section. Do you know what it's like walking into the "chubby" section of a store? Once I had this teenage girl (skinny, of course) show me dresses. If I could have magically disappeared on the spot, believe me, I would have.

Anyway, my mom and I couldn't find anything that fit me. It was a disaster. We didn't talk very much on the way home.

The next day when I came home from school, Mom showed me five dresses she had bought for me. She told me I could pick out the one I liked best. Two of the dresses actually fit me! I had a choice! One was pink and the other was a light green. My mother said the light green dress brought out the green in my eyes. My eyes are kind of pretty, so I picked the green one. When I looked in the mirror, I didn't look too bad. Did I mention that I don't like full-length mirrors? I really like it much better when my mother brings clothes home for me. I wish she'd do that all the time.

Practically every day after school, I go over to the Happy Time Nursery School. The director, Miss Loretta, lets me be a helper. I just love going there.

This all started many months ago. I pass Happy Time Nursery School on my way home from school and the playground faces the street. When I walk by, the kids are always playing outside. I used to stop at the fence and talk to the children. Before I knew it, I was singing with them. Then I started telling them jokes and making them laugh. I'm a pretty good joke-teller. Do you know what time it is when an elephant sits on your fence? It's time to get a new fence! That really cracks up the kids.

After I started doing that, one day Miss Loretta asked, "Would you please come into my office?"

"Okay," I said. I was really afraid she was going to ask me not to bother the kids anymore.

She said, "I can tell you really like little children. What's your name?"

"Dolly," I told her. I was still waiting to hear her tell me not to talk to the children anymore.

"Dolly, you may come inside and visit the children on your way home from school. Would you like that?"

I could barely answer, I was so excited. "Oh yes, yes, I would love to, but first I have to ask my mother, and if she says it's okay I'll see you tomorrow."

That's how it all started, and I've been helping out at Happy Time, and it's my favorite thing to do. When I read the children stories, I act very dramatic. I change my voice and sometimes I make funny sounds, like when I tell the story of the three bears. I have a different voice for each character in the book.

All of the children like me a lot, and I love them, especially Angela. Angela is four years old and has big blue eyes. She's very pretty. Angela is blind. She has never seen a flower or a bird. She has never seen anyone. She is a very brave little girl and everyone likes her. She loves to sing and she really laughs hard at my jokes.

Last month Angela and all the four-year-olds had a graduation. They will be going on to kindergarten soon. The graduation was at night, so the parents didn't have to take time off from work. I was invited and my parents came with me.

After everybody got a certificate of graduation, little Angela walked up to the microphone (Miss Loretta helped her) and said, "I would like to ask Dolly to please come up on the stage. On behalf of the Happy Time Nursery School, I would like to give Dolly a special certificate."

I couldn't believe what I was hearing. Me? A special certificate? My parents looked over at me and just smiled extra big smiles. I didn't think anyone could smile that big at me. My legs were really shaking, but somehow I walked up onto the stage.

Miss Loretta put her arm around me and said, "Dolly has been a big help to our nursery school. She has given everyone a lot of love and made a lot of people very happy. We are proud to have Dolly with us, and we all want to thank her very much."

Then Angela handed me a great big certificate. I bent down to kiss her, and Angela whispered, "You are my most beautiful friend."

For the first time in a long, long time, I thought of myself as just plain Dolly, instead of Dolly the fat girl. That was one of the most wonderful moments of my life. It was the best day I ever had.

I want to tell you about my new friend, Beth. Beth is my neighbor. She just moved to our block a short time ago. She's married to Bob. They're very nice people. They both work, but on the weekends they're home a lot, and sometimes I visit. Bob is a big sports fan and Beth isn't, so sometimes when Bob goes to a ball game with his friends, Beth and I just sit and talk. We have become very good friends. Beth is twenty-six years old, very beautiful and very thin.

When we first got to know each other, I noticed that Beth always seemed to know what I was thinking. Without my telling her, she always knew exactly what was going on in my mind. For instance, one time I was wearing a new shirt and jeans. She told me that she liked my new outfit. Then she said, "Going shopping is probably not one of your favorite things to do."

I said, "No, it isn't," and I quickly started talking about something else.

Another time I mentioned Andrew, my brother, to her. She said, "I bet there are moments you love him a lot and at the same time you probably hate him because he is so thin." Once again I changed the subject. I was beginning to wonder if maybe Beth had a crystal ball or something, but I didn't say anything.

One day when I went over to Beth's house she answered the door dressed in a leotard. It looked like she'd been working hard; she was sweating. She told me she had been exercising and invited me to join her doing sit-ups.

"No thanks," I said. "I'll just sit here and watch."

"When I was your age," Beth said, "I never liked doing exercises. Is that how you feel, Dolly?"

I nodded but didn't say anything about it. We talked for awhile, and for some reason I began to do some sit-ups with her. I didn't feel embarrassed. And although it was not so easy, it was sort of fun. In fact, we both started laughing.

The following week I saw Beth wearing a sweat suit, and she asked me if I would like to go jogging with her. After what happened in Mr. Dobson's gym class during relay races, I promised myself I would never run again. I wanted to tell Beth that I felt like a bowl of Jello when I ran, but instead I said, "No. I've got something else to do."

Once, however, I was walking down the street, and again along came Beth in her sweat suit. She was jogging so slowly that she seemed to be gliding along on air. She stopped running and walked with me. We began to talk, and pretty soon we were walking faster and faster, and then I was slowly jogging with her. We began to laugh when we both realized that I was running even though I don't like to run.

I'm still not crazy about exercising or jogging, but I've started doing it and it's become fun. When I used to exercise, I would always get hungry, but when I do it with Beth I don't think about food. I told Beth about that, and she said it's because I decided to do it, not because anyone told me to.

I've always exercised or dieted because Mom or the doctor or someone told me to do it. When I exercise with Beth, it's because I want to and no one has pushed me into it. Sometimes when people try to make me do things, I do the opposite on purpose, even if deep down I know what they're saying is for my good. It's just that everyone is always telling me what to do so I'll get thin, and it never really works.

After many weeks of running and exercising with Beth, she said to me, "Dolly, you really have helped me a lot with my exercising and jogging because if you didn't do it with me I probably would have quit."

"Me? — help you? I think it's the other way around!" I said.

"What do you mean, Dolly?" Beth asked.

"How come you say things out loud at the same time I am thinking them inside. You seem to read my thoughts and know how I feel."

Beth said, "Maybe it's because we are so much alike, almost like twin sisters."

I said, "Are you kidding? Twin sisters? Why, I must weigh more than you, and I'm only ten. When I'm your age, I'll probably weigh twice as much as you."

"You know, Dolly, since you've been exercising, I think you've lost some weight."

I explained to her that I'd lost weight before but always put it right back on.

She said maybe this time I wouldn't, and anyhow it really wasn't important because the time would come when I would lose weight and keep it off forever.

I laughed at her. But I felt like crying, too. I knew that could never be true. I thought she was my friend, and here she was telling me fairy tales.

I was about to say that I had to leave when she suggested I look at a photo album. Terrific, I thought. Who wants to see her wedding pictures? Didn't she realize she had upset me and that I might not be her friend again—EVER?

Beth placed the album on the table in front of me. The pictures had been taken a long time ago. First it showed a baby, and then the same girl got older and older and bigger and bigger. I saw myself in that girl. She was as fat as me. Then the girl was even a fat teenager. I began to recognize something familiar about her. It was the look on her face that was familiar, the smile. Then I knew. IT WAS BETH! I couldn't mistake that smile. She had been fat just like me. This thin, beautiful woman, my friend Beth, had been like me—just like me!

She told me all about how she felt when she was a little girl. She told me that all her friends had been thin and that the boys made fun of her. It was almost as if she was talking about my life.

I used to believe that I was the only person in the world who felt the way I did. It was so good to know I wasn't alone.

Beth said that the time came for her when she wanted to be thin, not for her mother, not to please her school friends, not because she was told to, but because she wanted to do it for herself.

She said the time will come for me when I will like myself so much that I won't ever want to be fat again. When that happens, food won't be very important anymore. She asked me how I felt when I helped out at the nursery school. She asked me if I thought about food when I was there. You know, I honestly did not think about how I looked or if I was hungry. Beth said that's the beginning…She said the time might be when I'm eighteen (that's when it happened with Beth) or fifteen or thirteen or even now. She said only I could make that decision.

I'm so lucky I have Beth as a friend. It's important to have someone who understands.

For the first time I really feel like everything is going to be all right some day. Ever since I've gotten to know Beth and the kids at the nursery school I've been feeling a lot better about myself. I know now that some day, when I'm ready, I'll be thin…maybe I'm ready now!

Bill and Enid Bluestein live in Studio City, California, with their children. Bill graduated in psychology from University of California at Los Angeles and received a law degree from Southwestern University. For the past ten years, he has taught and lectured throughout the United States and Canada, sharing his own knowledge and experience after losing over seventy pounds and maintaining his weight loss.

He has written numerous articles for newspapers and other periodicals and has appeared on radio and television talk shows with such well-known personalities as Michael Jackson and Phil Donahue.

Enid is a graduate of the University of Arizona and has taught school in Los Angeles, Chicago, and Tucson. She has been an associate producer and research editor for radio and television productions, including one which was nominated for an Emmy and received the Golden Mike award. She also is an aspiring songwriter.

Susan Kennedy, illustrator and graphic designer, lives in Minneapolis. She attended Minneapolis College of Art and Design. In the past year she has illustrated two other books, Hatch! by Karyn Henley and The Story of Arachne by Pamela Espeland, both Carolrhoda books from Lerner Publications.